Will You Share With Me?

Walter Rinder

Will You Share With Me?

CELESTIAL ARTS
MILLBRAE, CALIFORNIA

Copyright©1975 by Celestial Arts

Published by CELESTIAL ARTS, 231 Adrian Road,
Millbrae, California 94030

First Printing: October, 1975
Manufactured in the United States of America

Library of Congress Cataloging in Publication Data

Rinder, Walter.
        Will you share with me?

        I.   Title.
PS3568.I5W5   811'.5'4   75-9081
ISBN 0-89087-072-1

    2 3 4 5 6 7 8 9 10 − 80 79 78 77 76

I dedicate this book to "Love"
who has taught me to like myself

PART I

THE SHADOW
OF
THE MOUNTAIN

SIMPLE THINGS

I have come to know the simple things in life
that help to make the complex mind silent of many
frustrations.

the sound of leaves
the knocking on my door of a friend
a forest illuminated by the moon
the smell of fireplace smoke as I walk down
the road
a frog hiding in the foliage with her family
picking huckleberries from the bushes
making rose hip tea from wild roses
finding sour grass and mushrooms for a salad
waking up to the sound of a river
eating homemade bread baked in my kitchen
building a woodshed beneath the pines
discovering new flowers
finding old things in a homestead
feeling the earth . . . breathing

VARIETY

Continuity in shades of green
the formation of design
shapes that blend into the whole
a pleasant touch upon the mind

Continuity in types of people
the formation of our kind
races that blend into the whole
a gift to inspire mankind

EARTHEN FLOOR

amidst the trees and mountains
                    and sloping edges
the life filled splendor of
                    these natural hedges
whose hands of wind, whose hands
                    of rain
molded and sculptured this
          magnificent terrain
man out here is something more
than tiny seeds placed
          upon this earthen floor

THE GREAT WHITE MOUNTAIN

We hiked all morning up the slope of the mountain, through the cover of trees, to the top. Sitting on the top we looked over the ridges, into the valleys which separated these giant mounds of earth.

The Indians once sat on this very spot worshiping the Great Spirit, honoring the season of their hunt, for this was their hunting ground. A time when bear roamed in vast numbers eating the huckleberries and catching salmon and steelhead trout in the radiant streams and rivers that wound their way through the corridor that led to the Great White Mountain. Deer and beaver were plentiful, as were the ducks and grouse and pheasants. There was plenty for all, for life was in balance. The predator sought out his prey and the prey would many times evade the predator. As things died, new life was born upon the mountains and the balance continued. Then one day the white man entered this domain. The Great White Mountain accepted him with suspicion for the mountain had seen what the white man had done to the lands in the east.

More and more men came and as they came they began to plunder and rape, taking advantage of the hospitality that the Great White Mountain offered them in her bounty. They began to strip her naked, cutting down the trees, catching the beaver and bears for fur, shooting the deer and ducks.

Now, a hundred years later, the Great White Mountain can be seen weeping, for she has witnessed the destruction of balance in her domain. Most of her beautiful creatures are gone and a very few old trees stand to tell the tale of the white man's ax and saw.

As I sat upon this rock, my eyes scanning the countryside, I too felt the shame and sorrow of what man had done, for all the beauty of nature that I would never see, or feel, nor would my children. I looked up toward the Great White Mountain feeling a small degree of the pain she must feel, watching her children destroyed. I got up and walked over to a clump of wildflowers and bent down to kiss them and the tears fell from my eyes upon their petals and at that moment the earth began to tremble and the clouds began to swirl faster, and the wind swept down between the mountains, and I felt the Great White Mountain saying:

> *What has been ravished by your people can never be reclaimed, my son, but you can protect what little remains so that once again beauty shall inherit the earth.*

IN THE SHADOW OF THE MOUNTAIN

In the shadow of the mountain
there lived a boy of a restless age
neither time nor people could hold him
always moving to another phase

In the shadow of the mountain
he found bits of love but couldn't stay
a home or promises wouldn't keep him
nor things that people, to him, would say

In the shadow of the mountain
he built his life near the river's bend
lived each day in hopes and searching
never sure his searching would ever end

In the shadow of the mountain
he controlled his patience night and day
but soon his restlessness would find him
then one early morning he drifted away

In the shadow of the mountain
as the buds of spring appear
those that knew him held the memory
of his dreams held in a lonely sphere

Of a boy who touched the sunlight
cradled love within his hands
wanting only to love people
in his vast enchanted land

THE FIRST SNOWFALL

This morning I awoke earlier than usual for some unknown reason, sat up in bed and looked out the window to see what kind of day it was going to be. What to my amazement should appear but a snow dressed wonderland. I guess that's why I must have awakened so early, not to miss any of this special day. I quickly got dressed and went outside to explore this most welcome of visits from the heavens.

I saw the slender branches of the maple trees holding many little snow puffs. The cedar and hemlock trees were laden with large patches of white powder, their branches bowing to the audience of nature. Even some of the rust and yellow leaves of the vine maple held their autumn hue, peeking their faces out from their new environment; a thousand smiles everywhere I went.

It was early and as of yet there were neither tire tracks nor footprints, except mine. I felt sad as I walked down the road marring the smooth untouched surface of the snow.

Flakes were floating down from the clouds, landing on my nose, my cheeks, my eyelashes as I looked upward, thanking my creator for this wonderful experience, and for my eyes to see and my skin to feel sensations and my ears, to hear the earth and my nose to smell life's growth and my heart to feel happy.

COMMUNICATING WITH NATURE

have you ever communicated with nature?
the trees were the first I related to
not with words...which so often have a multitude
　　of meanings and can be misinterpreted
but with greater direction I tell them of my
　　　　feelings by
running my hand over their bark and sometimes
singing one of my poems to them or
tickling the leaves on the branches
they laugh, you know, kinda like people
I've watched them die from overcrowding or
a storm blow them down
or a disease kill them from inside
kinda like people
the strong survive
to know the dawn of another day
kinda like people

SENSES

In the woods my senses have become extremely alert to the sounds and smells, many strange to me.

One day while exploring near a waterfall I found a beautiful clump of mushrooms hiding in a dead log.

I had discovered another link in the universal chain of life which binds us together.

A NEW PART OF LIFE

The sun is disappearing behind the trees across the river and the shadows are getting long. There is a playful breeze coming through the open door behind me. It is a good feeling sitting here in my mountain home writing this to you.

When you come to visit me I can now share a more meaningful world with you, for I have learned more of myself from my new environment, and now must live that life feeling new growth. Living in nature has caused me to look into myself for the many answers to the many questions I have looked to man to answer for me. From man I received only answers that could not satisfy the feeling of truth that my soul demanded.

So the new parts of me you will have to get to know for they will be strange to you as you knew me before. Allow time to mellow this unknown portion of me and you will find comfort and security in my words and actions. Your understanding of me will bring us closer together.

As we change from the brush strokes of encounters, my friend, we blend into a canvas of the world the great artist imagined.

PART II

LEARNING
LOVE

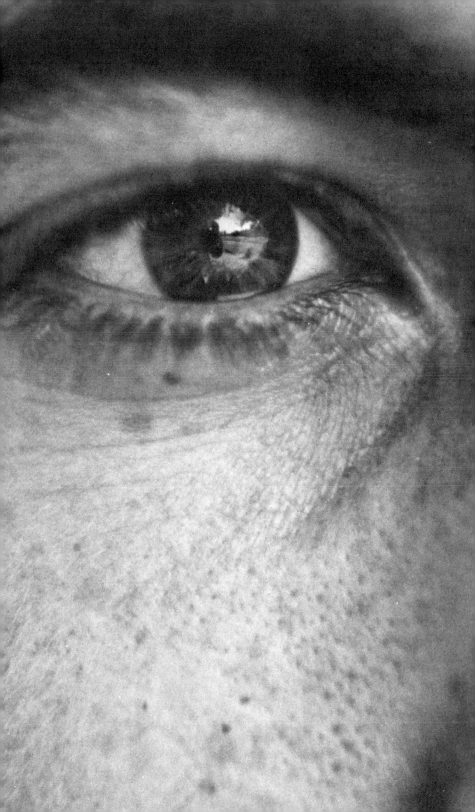

LEARNING FROM YOU

I want to learn from you by becoming a part of your life. Within your eyes I see mirrored many experiences which have given you insight into yourself, channels I wish also to explore. By being yourself you show me all the things I wish to be but am not.

THE PUPPET

life's music began
as the puppet walked upon the stage
held by the master's hands
do what I command, my little wooden friend
the puppeteer grunted
I gave you life
and by these strings
only shall you live
when the audience
finds you tiresome
I will cut your strings
and discard you
to the pile of trash
for I will need you no more
so be of good use to me
as you live
that coins shall
jingle in my pocket

       now a puppet is a puppet
         and a puppet has no choice
       but you, my friend are human
         and with this you can rejoice

YOUR MUSIC

the cry of your spirit
echoed through the strains
as your fingers picked the
strings of your heart
running the fields
with you
we threw our dreams
to the wind
as night's shroud
protected our serenity
deeper we plunged
into each other
our shells becoming
transparent rays of the sun
your music rolled toward me
coming to rest
within me
like the waves crashing
with thunderous energy
to rest in the arms of the sand
. . . this is called love!

THE CAPACITY OF LOVE

The capacity of love is only stifled
by our lack of experience
as the bird who sits in the nest
until it learns to fly
one of our greatest joys
is to be a new experience
to another person . . . for love
has many faces

JUSTIFICATION

Your existence no longer has to be justified, nor do those feelings you hold inside, either to yourself or to others. Just your striving to live, the focus being your true self though much of your life may seem out of focus, is justification

. . . without explanation

BECOME RICH

You may be poor in possessions
but you can become rich in your
ability to experience the essence of life

possessions get old
break
wear out
time weakens their use
and are many times discarded
but the experience of love
is a person's greatest asset
which endures the years.

EMOTIONS

Cannot be commanded
or directed, for the only
authority is our willingness
to understand ourselves
reacting to the moods
which give each person
their individual identity

MANY WAYS TO LEARN

Friendship becomes deep when virtuous men learn to love the good in one another and understand the bad which clutters the mind . . . for virtue gives more joy than the physical plane of beauty, being untouched by time.

YOU LIFTED ME

Naked with only God's cover
I was lifted above the earth
you carrying me toward the water
as the waves ran to meet us
our warm skin rubbing with
a sensual softness
your muscles in rhythm
to your purpose
a protective coating
for the long journey
as you walked on top
of the water's crest
I rested my cheek
under the curvature
of your chin, calm,
knowing your footsteps
would lead us
to a place beyond
where creating love
was the reason
for our journey

When love fills your heart
fear finds no home

LOVE IS NOT A SOUND

Love is not a sound
often times spoken in haste
or promises you intend not to keep
or a walk down a one way street

Love is hope where hope was once severed
            from your mind
Love is living each moment with the person
            of love you find
Love is trust when trust repeatedly stole
            from your life
Love is never giving up when you're despondent
            or in strife
Love is seeing all you can
in each and every man
'tis not a sound
that makes love profound

LEARNING LOVE

To the Mother of Nature was born a child
                    naked to man thoughts
and she wrapped him in innocence
                    for mankind was cruel
and she nursed him with compassion
                    for mankind was harsh
and the child suckled from her breasts
          of kindness and goodness
          for mankind was selfish
and he began to grow and to learn
and his feet began to feel the humid soil
and his hands began to feel his sensitive body
and his eyes began to see the wonder of
                              living things
and his ears began to hear the harmonious sounds
                    of the creatures
and his nose began to smell the aroma of life
and he was curious
and he started to roam
and he started to explore
and he started to absorb
and he became involved
and he grew and he learned

and Mother Nature watched with great pride
and he felt the thorns of the berry bushes
                        from which he ate
and he felt the sting of the bee from which
                        he obtained honey
and he felt the sharp edges of broken branches
                        of the trees he used to build his home
and he felt the pain of fire, when touched, he
                        used for warmth
and he felt the discomfort of certain plants
                        from which he sought to derive food
and he learned to respect all forms of life
and he learned what not to touch
and he learned what was not good for him
and he learned to be careful yet not afraid
and he learned the difference of each
and he felt good
and he learned and he grew
and he began to see himself as a part of all he saw
and he took from life only what he needed
and he took from life only what was good
and he became a part of the balance
and he cared about all he saw
and he grew and he learned
and he helped the weaker in Nature
and he honored the stronger in Nature
and he saw life and death in harmony
and he knew he was being taught
and he saw continuity
and he saw simplicity
and he saw humility
and he saw wisdom
and he learned and he grew

and he saw families of things
and he saw them caring about each other
and he saw them sharing with each other
and he saw them fulfilling their purpose
and he began to look for his own kind
and he began to yearn for a family
and he grew and he learned
and he searched
and he experienced
and he contemplated
and one day he found his own kind
and he wanted to relate
and he entered his family in innocence
and he gave of himself with compassion
and he was filled with kindness and goodness
and he communicated in a language called love
and his body was motivated by the expression
of love
and he told his people how he had learned
and he was spontaneous in love
and he was deliberate in love
and how he appeared to be what he was
and how he had grown from the guidance
of his Mother, Nature
and his family thought him strange
and his family thought him different
and he asked . . . was there any other way to be!

PART III

THE CITY

I COME

you are the night
I am the sun
I chose to walk
you chose to run
you are the millions
I am but one
I search for love
you offer fun
I give my heart
you disclose none
you are tall buildings
between them I come
you are the night
I am the sun

THE DARKNESS

a boy or girl alone
standing on the corner waiting for an
acknowledgment from a passing car
a boy or girl alone
following shadows down a busy street
a boy or girl alone
from a hotel window watching life
a boy or girl alone
who takes a ten for an hour of pretending
a boy or girl alone
whose eyes reveal the pills

ornaments upon your city streets
neither fools nor kings can see
the image of belonging
that surrounds them
nor light of day erase
the need to become a part of . . .
so absent in their longing

CITY DWELLERS

your first responsibility is to yourself
tend to your own body
        that it may serve you well
tend to your own mind
        that it may take you beyond
then offer your imagination as a gift
your knowledge as a lesson
your wisdom as a virtue
        without obligation
        without reward
        without restitution

that our youth may become
the living statues sculptured for a
                        better world

The creator gave you a voice
 . . . other creatures may suffer in silence

MY ATTIC

'tis not for you I shed my tears
but for that part of me
that always is alone
when my eyes are dry
all those forgotten people
whom I loved
are put back on the dusty shelves
of memories
my attic that created tears
the door once more closed
until another time
where thought and deed
leads up the stairs to
tears of things
that passed me by
someday, no more
will enter that cobwebbed room
where sorrow is the air I breath
and torment my only light

COLLECTING MOMENTS

In our glory and defeat
the moments of life repeat
    as faces are collected in our mind
for but a rapid span of time
when two souls can intertwine
    infatuation is the treasure they find

Can these moments all endure
that this love may feel secure
    when the time be just the hours
        of one night?
collecting moments with different ones
may be why he always runs
    where with one, the years bring
        moments of delight
        and peaceful nights

YESTERDAY

do your eyes betray
the sad and lonely times
of yesterday
when one small word
hello!
could have replaced the sorrow
with a smile upon your face

sensitive love
could have lifted your body
from the blacktop streets
the carnival buildings
those fickle signs
promising thrills and chances
substitutes for love

one night of affection
might have soothed
your longing
until another time
your feet are tired
the cold wind
forces you inside
to a bed of isolation

tomorrow is another day
should you awake
with joyful eyes
in hopes that love
will come a calling
with but a simple word
hello!

DANNY

Grew up with mother and brother on a ranch
                              in California
they scratched the land for subsistence
poor in possessions . . . rich in health and simplicity
the boy of seventeen I met was a wild youth
        abounding with endless energy
        challenging life at every opportunity
        every animal, every blade of grass
                              was his friend
for the first time he came to the city
        living with me for many months
the city became confusing, cluttered
people's words and motives became hurts he
                        didn't understand
his innocence was challenged
he began to question my kindness, my love
        when men of folly would interpret to him
                        my motives as a lie
so he ran away, back to the country, to the trees
        and stream and animals he knew
a few years later I saw him again in his
        environment and he spoke these words to me

In your city I became a slave to man's greed and
was overwhelmed by his flattery and lustful
persuasion and did not hear the voice of my soul
and still with all the pain I caused, you came back
as my friend. Will you stay that I may learn your
ways? It seems our voices within are the same.

YOUR REACH

There are two worlds
chose the best of each
undertake to spend your time
they're both within your reach.

TWO DIFFERENT WORLDS

two different worlds of sea and steel
but only one is free
the other chokes with iron bars
and cluttered humanity

two different worlds of birds and man
existing side by side
in time will one overcome
the other which has died!

YOU, MY CITY

How you pull me apart with your instability, with your inconsistency for I never know what your moods will be from day to day. You never will make a commitment that we might build together. Sometimes you surround me with affection and other times with indifference, as if you don't know me. I can take your hurting me, I can take the struggles, I can endure the pain but I cannot take your indifference.

For three years I have been courting you, trying to develop a relationship whereby I cared to stay. Maybe we could even live together building a home, a family of people. But time has shown me you are fickle with many lovers and you chose me when your need arose, not concerned that I had needs also—that I might want to plant roots and belong to your family, even though I be only one of your lovers. I accepted that fate.

You teased me when I first met you and promised things you could not fulfill. It took all this time for me to realize . . . Love was a game in which you made up the rules to suit your purpose. When I wouldn't play you ignored me. I still tried for I loved you, with hope, with devotion, and gave all I knew of myself and then gave what I newly learned from you. Still it was not enough.

So I am leaving you, maybe forever, maybe for awhile. I must travel to other places where I may find civilization in need of what life has made of me.

PART IV

THAT YOU
MAY
KNOW OF ME

WHAT IT IS TO BE HUMAN

I am sitting in the Portland Greyhound bus terminal, having a cup of coffee. Coffee is the remembrance, for me, of years gone by. The nectar of the gods afforded strangers for the time when all other words fail their lips. The hour is 10:30 at night. Darkness seems the time when the attic of one's mind is visited in search of some lost treasure, forgotten, as a lost love revived to what may have been, but wasn't. Outside the rain is pouring from the clouds like tears from love when it is alone. How sad is the rain tonight or maybe the rain is laughing tears of joy. I guess it depends where you are or where you have been.

A couple of hours ago I was sitting in my home up in the mountains, listening to the music of my past, within the comforts of my bedroom. The familiar things one collects over the years to keep reminding us of what once was. Gifts from people to bridge the heart. As I lay on my bed the music began to bring back memories of people and places I used to know. My thoughts became a cavern where the echos of the past bounced against every wall and ceiling of my mind. Faster and deeper came the penetration until the reality of the now became the reliving of the many yesterdays where hopes and dreams were the lights I followed from the blackness, where my feelings could not relate to the reality surrounding me or my heartbeat be heard by those close to me. Only in the distance of time was my soul illuminated, seeing the white peaks of truth as clear as crystal.

People who had touched my life; some for but a moment of living, some chose to stay a little longer before departing to another love. Some came back over the years to renew love's embrace, some cared to stay for awhile to tease the longing of my heart that they were my beloved come at last from my dreams. A few have developed friendships over the years which seem to have been built for a lifetime. Can friendship fill the space that is reserved for being in love?

For most I was a stepping stone when the waters of desire were too deep to ford: people I made love to in strange hotel rooms because we didn't have anywhere else to go, people who took from me all they needed in their hunger leaving me the bones and scraps to dine upon. People whose dry, barren soul I tilled, planting fields of love; then I was sent away before the time of harvest. People who shared their mind and body in intimacy with me for a night then forgot my name before their footsteps reached the streets. People who used me for their needs and wants until they found no longer a use, then smiled goodbye.

. . . people who stole my time, absorbed my knowledge, experimented with my being, syphoned my generosity, then disappeared into the mass of humanity, becoming the past that, on lonely nights such as this, would cause my restlessness to increase its search for whatever would still my flesh and bones to a quiet bed of understanding; people who said they loved me meaning they were in love with the idea of being in love; people who used my friendship, my companionship to kill time instead of time to live; people who thought sex was love and bed was home; people who gave to me because they believed in what I was trying to make of my life; people who loved me as I was without trying to change me; people who gave love to me from the feelings of their heart not the lust of their minds; people who truly wanted to become a part of my life; people who wanted to increase their capacity to love and were willing to step into the unknown with me; people who were not afraid to show you they cared; people who gave more of themselves in a few encounters than most can in years.

. . . people I picked out of the gutter of life; people I held when no one else cared; people I sat with when the world was spinning around them; people I took from the cold indifferent city streets and warmed their bodies and their minds in my home; people who had given up on life until I gave them a reason to care, a motivation, a purpose to continue; people who carried weapons of pain I substituted with tools of love; people in whose faces I always saw the image of love and myself falling in love with those faces over and over again until my world became a forest of faces with blond hair, black hair, a face with sad eyes, a face with a straight nose, a face with a scar, a face with a square chin, a face with bright cheeks, a face with a beard, a face with soft skin, a face with sensitive eyes, a face with smile wrinkles, a face serenely bound, a face of strength, of compassion, of classical beauty, of simple thoughts.

. . . Faces I wanted to give love to, minds I wanted to enter, bodies I wanted to explore bringing them the riches of touch and affection beyond their imagination that would make gold crumble to dust, jewels become as dull as a gray sky.

. . . becoming one as the romantic rhythm of the sea, the poetic words of the soul, the rebirth of the human spirit.

Places with high mountains, desert sands, miles of ocean beaches, pine and cedar forests, groves of cyprus trees, rose garden backyards, tulip beds and morning glory fences, an old swing on a wooden front porch, a park on a summer night, a haystack in a barnyard, a campfire by a lake, a cabin by highway 101, a basement of a Victorian house in San Francisco, a Y.M.C.A. room in Phoenix, an apartment in Dallas, a barn in northern California, a house in Pittsburgh, a room in Portland, a trailer in Los Angeles, a hotel in Tulsa, a camper in Maine, a street in New York, a diner in Lexington, a campsite in the redwoods, small towns and large cities, country roads and fast freeways began to merge as one as the flood of memories engulfed the spaces of my mind. The years began to pass like an autumn wind blowing the leaves from the tree of my life until it was stripped bare. I stood naked but the wind kept blowing, bending the branches of my naked soul and for a moment I felt as if I would be uprooted by its force. So I jumped up from the bed and drove the forty miles into Portland hoping to find another face that might still my restless soul. Maybe this time there would be no separation and the memories we would share together.

It has been several hours as I have been sitting here in the bus station writing this. Most of the people who were here when I arrived are gone now, except for the girl with a newborn baby (what kind of world will it find), a lady with a shopping bag whose face mirrored her smiling a lot, a young man wearing an army uniform which seemed out of place, an old man who misplaced his hat and overcoat but later found them, and a young girl who was sitting alone until a young man asked if he might join her (when she got up to refill her coffee cup he looked at me with a smile for she was very pretty).

How many bus stations have I sat in all over the country. And for how many reasons have I been brought into their domain. Listening to the loudspeaker announcing places where people lived out their lives or at least a part of them. Some to me were a memory and others unknown. Here I am back again, a restless traveler of the universe, who travels on wishes walking upon an illusion that is real, that love, someday, will come to stay. Will reality be so kind as to grant me safe passage through the time barrier?

I have grown from youth to manhood and still, for whatever reason eludes me, my dreams still seem to stay intact. My motivation continues to steer the course of my destiny over the roughest of waters even though the land of hope at times seems far away.

The coffee shop is closing and the next bus doesn't leave till morning. So back out in the city I will head and sometime soon write of times and places and people who become a part of my past, of my feelings, of my learning what it is to be human.

SHENANDOAH VALLEY

blue water winds itself
around autumn's
browns and golds
like the ribbon
of a package
truly it was a gift
given to man by God

as I wandered down
from the Blue Ridge Mountains
my eyes beheld
this spot of earth
nature has been kind
to this valley
for beauty was abundant
quaint little farms
nestled on the knolls
among the stately trees
naked now
sunshine warming the day
bringing together the colors
in harmonious patterns
clouds, the minstrels of the sky
singing songs of bygone days
the sun rose three times
before I journeyed on
to other places
where people lived out
their lives
I, still searching
for where I belonged

THE FREE SPIRIT OF THE WIND

I knew a place where the wind blew free
and branches hung down in tatters
where I used to gaze into the morning haze
contemplating what really matters

I knew a place where my thoughts ran free
and the day seemed to hang suspended
where the earth and my flesh intermeshed
and my awareness was extended

THE PIANO

I sat in the Harvard University common room
listening to the vibrant music of my friend as he
played the grand piano; sounds pirouetting back
and forth, touching the high walnut ceiling and
carved wooden walls, waltzing in and out of the
arched windows. The black silhouetted trees stood
motionless outside listening to his performance.

The music he played paralleled the grandeur
of the old ornate furniture which stood within the
room, telling of times and relationships and of
young men who would find greatness beyond this
school of learning, who sat in these very chairs
listening to their friend playing the piano, as I was
at that very moment. Paintings hanging on the
walls created by well-known artists of their times,
of men who have contributed to the growth and
destiny of our lives. I felt I was reliving history, my
imagination running rampant with the events that
happened here on these grounds. Young men who
felt the same enchantment and inspiration I was
feeling as my friend echoed the great composers,
my mood being changed by Bach, Beethoven,
Strauss, Brahms as they spoke of their lives and
loves. An aura of people of past and present com-
pleting the now as I lived each timeless moment.

My friend, his long curly blond hair, white
turtleneck sweater, construction boots and maroon
pants with a hole in the knee making his feelings
known; a long-haired hippie sitting at the grand
piano at Harvard University playing for me what
his lips could not speak or his body accept, only in
the communication his fingers manifested as they
ran over the keys sounding through the great halls
of this university on one summer night in June.

REFLECTIONS

I am what I am as my past reflects
what life has chiseled me
just as this rock's fragments fall
from the pounding of the relentless sea

There's a time to act, a time to dream
and a time to understand
that nothing ever stays the same
neither rock, nor shore, nor man

Someday the rock will be no more
someday I too will cease
but not before I build my dream
then my soul, from my flesh, can be released

WHEN LOVE ARRIVES

I want to be unattached
from mankind's inability
to give from the soul
free from man's restraints
I wish
to recapture my own soul
my youthful dreams
to make love to you
to make love to people
to make love to the world

feel the sand between my toes
the sun at my fingertips
the clouds in my hair
the flowers in my eyes
the wind in my veins
the summer meadows in my heart

feel the hands of love
upon my skin
feel the sensual beauty of love
when love arrives

A PART OF LOVE

Real to me is my lover
yet a fantasy, misplaced
yet a dream, unfulfilled
displaced in the antiquity
of another time . . . another civilization

I, a man of gentle thoughts
never to dishonor
a friendship in love
who seeks truth
peeking from behind
the curtains of man's limitations
man, the actor, the role player
the egocentric director

I dream, idealistically, romantically, sexually
that love will awake me by its presence
and I will sleep by its touch
awakened often by the screams
of man's fears
his moralistic justice
his insensitivity to himself

Love stands upon
the throne of youth
a prince of his age
his naked body
exploring the sensuality
of God's lighted world
of a time when love was grand
love was honored . . . exalted
above all else
valor lived in deeds
sharing was the creed
courage built walls of strength
against the demons of men's hearts

where boy and man gave love wings
soaring in and out
of the purity
of the boundless energy
of the eternal spirits
of the universe
making love was the oasis
in the desert of civilization

In truth I know of a boy
of reality
living in the world of now
of flesh and blood and bones
love flows from my veins
spilling from my heart
yet is channeled into an illusion
of another time
when we explored life's mysteries
sailing between the pillars of Hercules
learning in the great library of Alexandria
sitting together . . . listening to each others
words, thoughts, touch
which led us up
the mountain of knowledge
over the maze of barriers
to the pinnacle of oneness

today, we say hello
talking away time
in trifle utterances
meaningless phrases
space between us always
uncertainty our standard barrier

But in a yesteryear
he listened to my words
as if to the beating of his own heart
he followed me into the unknown
to a known awareness
to countries and places and sensitivity
that few men have ever dreamed of
that few men have ever imagined

he is the son of the sun
brother of the stars
child of eternity
student of the earth
music of the beloved
lover of love
he lives in my suffering
extends from my loneliness
emerges in my torment
is the image in a dream
he is part of my illusion
and part of my reality

because I am human

A LONG JOURNEY

I am very tired and weak from my long journey
Would you carry my belongings for awhile!
I have not much, just a broken heart that I
will have to mend, a cloak of courage
that is worn and dusty that I will need to
cleanse, and my boots of hope that have protected
my footsteps through life's brambles which need resoling
May I rest within your home a short while to do
those mentioned things before I start on my
journey's way?

WRITTEN TO A FRIEND

don't run away
because you expect from me
that which is you
your small world
can become overcrowded
feelings need space to grow
let our world expand
without boundaries
without fences
without cement fortresses
without those substitutes
which detain our participating
in this expansion

TAKE A FRESH BREATH OF LIFE

Fill your living parts
with a new vitality
of faith and determination
for they are both
born from the same womb

instead of accepting
things as they are
change things
like you wish they were
to the best of your ability
for anything is possible
when you
take a fresh breath, of life

FREEDOM   means
knowing you have free choice!

SPONTANEOUS

The apple ripens
as nature spontaneously gives
what is needed
to its maturing

human love is spontaneous
if it waits in its giving
the longer it waits
the less its chance
of maturing the ripening
of universal love

TO MY _____

I would rather hurt you myself, in your learning
from me of life and love, than see someone or
something else crush your will to live.

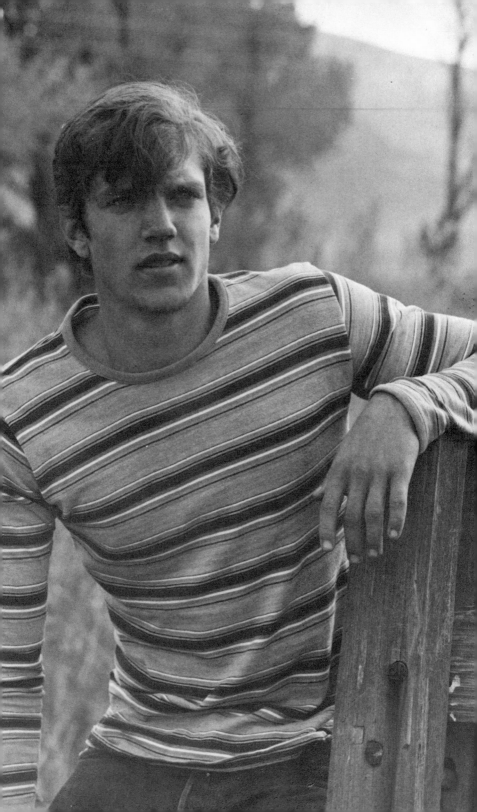

CONDEMNATION

Be hesitant in your condemnation of others
as their charity creates within you
                              expectations
as their love creates within you
                              animosity
as their presumptions create within you
                              suspicion
as their interpretation creates within you
                              disbelief
as their spontaneity creates within you
                              fear
what they feel is not man-made judgments
only the soul can understand the soul
                    . . . children know!

ASK ME

A young girl asked me, why do you write?
I replied,
Why is it that you sleep and eat?
She replied,
I sleep when I am tired and need rest and
eat when I feel hungry.
I replied,
Does not a farmer rest upon the bed of the
earth and satisfy his hunger ploughing his
fields?
Does not a poet rest in the bed of his
thoughts and satisfy his hunger with words?

FRIEND OR LOVER

should I try to love you
as we be lovers
and if love fails
will we grow away from each other
or should I stay and accept
the pieces and parts that are together
as in friendship
in hopes someday
they may become whole
rather then take the chance
of starting all over again
with someone else
later finding
we didn't try hard enough
now the pieces have scattered
we have stood too long
on the desert of
being alone

POTENTIAL

I feel a greater depth
of love
for what you can become
than what you are
now . . .
my perception
of your potential
is limitless
therefore as you grow
expand your feelings
so the fullness
of our love expands also
as the naked vine
which lies dormant
will become the beauty
of the bougainvillea

THAT I MAY KNOW OF YOU

Stranger
    to the life I've lived
stranger
    to the love I'd gladly give
yes speak, oh speak . . . speak
    make that lovely sound
    that I may know of you

stranger
    speak a gentle phrase or two
stranger
    I will stop to answer you
yes speak, oh speak . . . speak
    make that lovely sound
    that I may know of you

stranger
    talk of love and love will surely stay
stranger
    talk of fear and I will send it far away
yes speak, oh speak . . . speak
    make that lovely sound
    that I may know of you

stranger
    say your needs that they freely may be
              known
stranger
    and I will fill those needs as they,
           to me, are shown
yes speak, oh speak . . . speak
    make that lovely sound
    that I may know of you

FOR ME

to speak of love
to speak this exalted feeling
to speak these sacred words
      "I love you"
    is who I am
for you it means only to share that which
you feel is a part of you, for I will
accept all you have to give . . .
hoping because
      "I love you"
my example through my actions
may inspire your motivation in wanting
to give more in this sharing of love

      you have asked me
    where will I learn who I am!
     the answer lies in
      "I love you"

Sitting by the banks of the Sandy River early this
fall morning, when the sun was still behind the
ridge—my friend was looking out over the
waters—I watching his face becoming more
distinguishable as dawn approached realizing as I
watch that face . . .

  It isn't who you love
  or how you love
  It's just that you love

PART V

WHEN ALL HAS BEEN SAID

WORDS

There was a time when I believed in all words. This time being when I was young. I would listen, believing. Over the years my ears have become calloused and somewhat deaf to the words, false to the heart from which they spoke. I cried, often in silence from the hurts. But the wounds would soon heal, the scab disappears, leaving only a scar to remind me. Now I listen with my eyes.

POETS, WHO WILL COME AFTER HIM

His legacy found its roots in the poems his heart
had created. When flesh and bones vanish, as life
demands, what will be said of him. Will poets
speak praise upon their lips of a man who was the
shepherd of love or judge him a fool who lived in
dreams sitting upon the clouds? Will the poets who
come after him be inspired by his legacy or laugh in
dismay at his trite and simple words? Maybe some
will say he cared to give all he knew, but his being
different was not the common, ordinary thing to
do. That he was crucified by his own truth.

Is he dead? ask the poets of tomorrow!

I YOU OUR PEOPLE

If I can feel secure in my changes
then I know life can truly become exciting

If words lead to actions
then you must learn to speak your feelings

Trust in feelings
they are the voices of our soul

Many people ask the question, why?
but not enough make the statement, why not!

GOING HOME

My ignorance follows my footsteps
until I journey into people's souls
for there I read the scrolls of the universe
I have just begun to learn
though a third of my life has passed
as I live
      I feel
         I am
            going home!

HERE I WATCH
        AND HERE I FEEL
                AND HERE I HOPE

AND FROM MY HEART I SEAL IT WITH A KISS

                GOOD NIGHT

WALTER RINDER

Walt is the personification of the troubadour within us all. He lives out our fantasies through his travels, his experiences, and those he meets along the way. We share the feelings through his writing.

"Hi, you look a little down—like to talk about it?" You turn and there's Walt, his warm smile demolishing the wall of loneliness. He's been alone and dejected in many different environments. He's seen the drop-outs, the street people, the flower children, the runaways, and he is as one with them.

Walt is the "successful" poet who never allowed his achievements to become part of his living. The restlessness that was born in Chicago, a Gemini, grew up in Southern California and dropped out of college to wander the country. He is "home" in a house he built along a river in a forest not far from Portland, Oregon.

He has channeled just enough energy in specific directions to become an accomplished poet, photographer, and artist. The balance of his boundless energy is carefully invested in life. Those who read this book will enjoy reading Walt's personal philosophy in *Love Is My Reason* and sharing his unique gifts in his numerous other books of poetry and prose.